To

_____

From

_____

Date

_____

Rainbow of Comfort

Copyright© 2019 Rainbow Promise Publishing Group

Compiled and edited by Ruth Ashcraft Munday

Cover and interior photos Copyright© 2016, 2017, 2018 and 2019
Ruth Ashcraft Munday

Ann's Heart Copyright ©2017 Ruth Ashcraft Munday and Julia Taylor Ebel

Cover design and interior artwork Copyright ©2019 Rebecca Roten

ISBN 978-0-578-56695-5

All rights reserved. No part of this publication may be reproduced or transmitted for commercial purposes, except for brief quotations in printed reviews, without written permission of the publisher.

Quotation reference and Bible permissions are listed on the last page of this book.

Published by Rainbow Promise Publishing Group, Horn Lake, Mississippi.

www.printninja.com

Printed in China.

Rainbow of Comfort

**God's Love Over You
During Difficult Times**

RAINBOW PROMISE
PUBLISHING GROUP

Acknowledgements

Special thanks to those who contributed devotional writings and to Rebecca Roten for giving so generously of her artistic talent.

Thank you to Brandon Roten for touching up the cover photo. You have all helped this book become a reality.

I am forever grateful for everyone's love and support during this process. I pray the Lord will use this book to bring comfort to those going through difficult times.

~Ruth Ashcraft Munday

To Our Beloved

Ann

Ann's Heart

Ann's heart is a glowing rainbow,
Shining with a zeal for life,
Enfolding, loving all around her,
Lighting darkness, not despair.

Ann's heart encircles loved ones—
Family, friends, community—
A selfless circle, always seeking
To serve others
With no bounds.

Ann's heart holds a rainbow of music,
Bursting forth in sounds of joy,
Hymns to God,
Songs of kindness,
Colorful notes of peace and love.

Ann's heart is a prism of wonder,
Reflecting joy
In simple things—
Violets, zinnias, buttercups,
Mountains, rivers, birds, and snow.

Ann's heart is a loving prism,
Spreading light through the world she loves.
Inspiring courage
In an arc of faith
And a hope of eternal peace.

~Ruth Ashcraft Munday
With Julia Taylor Ebel

Contents

Foreword xi
Preface...xiii
A Great Resurrection 3
A Life Built Upon The Rock...5
A Place For You...7
Approaching God With Freedom And Confidence........9
Bread That Satisfies 11
Broken And Crushed 13
Can And Will 15
Come..17
Cultivating The Fruits Of The Spirit 21
Denying Ourselves For Jesus 23
Departing Triumphantly..25
Do Not Be Afraid, Little Flock....................................27
Do Not Fear 29
Do Not Lose Heart 31
Doubt..33
Drawing Nigh To God...35
Everlasting Peace 39
Every Tear..41
Fear Not 43
Getting Through The Shadowy Places.......................45
God Is Good 47
God With Us 49
God's Love 51
God's Rainbow Covenant..53
Immediately 57
It's Okay...59
Lean Not On Your Own Understanding.....................61
Lessons From Zinnias..63
Letting Our Hearts Not Be Troubled 65
Listening For The Still Small Voice 67

Love Is Patient	69
My Precious Ann	71
Not A Spirit Of Fear	75
Our Heavenly Reward	77
Perpetual Prayer And Thanksgiving	79
Positive Ways To Channel Grief	81
Pray Without Ceasing, Giving Thanks	83
Proceeding On With Untenuous Tenacity	85
Set God's Love As A Seal	87
Small Acts Of Kindness	89
Some Trust In Chariots	93
The Gift Of Beauty	95
The Gift Of Song	97
The Gifts Of Strength And Peace	99
The Lord Is My Strength	101
The Peace Of God	103
The Promise Of Comfort	105
Today	107
True Friends	111
Wait For The Lord	113
Waiting In Expectation	115
We Will Recognize Them	117
What A Hope We Have	119
What Does God Look Like	121
Whelmed, But Not Overwhelmed	123
When There Are No Words	125

Foreword

Despite the miles that separated Ann Brown Ashcraft and me, she was my best friend from the day we met in 1986. In her final days, I was honored to spend time by her side, sharing fond memories and photos, reading poems to her, and simply being present. Even then, we had so much to share.

During those last days, Ann and her loving circle of family and friends were still teaching me what friendship means and challenging me to grow in compassion and wisdom in the face of pain and the ultimate genuine grief that came with her passing. Through this time, I was led to build connections, not to let them go. I am still growing because our paths crossed.

I was one of many who walked a similar path with Ann. Surely, we each grew stronger for that journey. These pages hold reflections by those persons who, in turn, want to share words of encouragement with others facing difficult times—for whatever reasons—
and with caregivers, friends, and nurturers. You, too, face challenges.

These words are gifts to you. May they offer insight, strength, and encouragement. May they offer hope, comfort, and peace. May they be blessings that assure you that you are not alone, and may they remind you of God's presence through your own journey.

~Julia Taylor Ebel

Preface

The God Of All Comfort

Praise be to the God and Father of our Lord Jesus Christ, the Father of compassion and the God of all comfort, who comforts us in all our troubles, so that we can comfort those in any trouble with the comfort we ourselves have received from God.
II Corinthians 1:3-4(NIV)

The inspiration for this devotional book came about from a beautiful double rainbow that appeared over the house where my mother, Ann, was receiving home hospice care. The day will be forever etched in our minds. We were looking out the bedroom window, through the misting rain. Out of nowhere, the clouds broke open, the sun began to shine and our "Rainbow of Comfort" appeared! We felt enveloped in God's love and it created a memory to treasure.

My family and I received other means of comfort, as well, through nature, visits from family and friends, scripture, prayer, and finding positive ways to channel our grief. God sends various forms of comfort during difficult times. He knows just how to soothe us when no one else can. It is our hope that, through these shared scriptures and heartfelt reflections, you will be able to receive God's comfort in your own life.

~Ruth Ashcraft Munday

On behalf of: my father, Lee Ashcraft, my sister, Betsy Ashcraft Walker, and all of the contributors who have shared their words of faith and encouragement in this book.

Rainbow of Comfort

If the Spirit of him who raised Jesus from the dead dwells in you, he who raised Christ from the dead will give life to your mortal bodies also through his Spirit that dwells in you.

Romans 8:11 (NRSV)

A Great Resurrection

As a pastor, I have been with many people as their lives have come to an end here on this earth. I have seen that for some, it was a sweet relief, while for others, it was agony. The biggest difference was that while some were in Christ, others were not. I always would talk to those who were leaving this world about their faith and how they felt about their life-ending situation. The way to be prepared for this is to have a relationship with Jesus Christ.

The life-threatening events that I have experienced, a serious accident and also cancer, have brought me closer to the Lord. His Spirit, living in me, provides me with all that I need to continue – whether in this life or in eternity. I am still living with my cancer and know one day it will ravage my body. I don't fear this nor do I shrink from it. I am in the Lord and the Lord is in me by the Spirit. I will die from this body, to be raised by the same Spirit into a new body. And this new body will never be sick, injured, hurt, or die. I will truly be home and freed forever from all the burdens of this earthly life!

Thank you, Lord, for the salvation you have provided; I eagerly anticipate our lives together in eternity. Amen. Be blessed!

~Bro. Ray Owens

As you come to him, the living Stone—rejected by men but chosen by God and precious to him—you also, like living stones, are being built into a spiritual house to be a holy priesthood, offering spiritual sacrifices acceptable to God through Jesus Christ.

1 Peter 2:4-5 (NIV)

A Life Built Upon The Rock

As curator of the DeSoto County Museum, I have row upon row of books that can tell me about the rocks in our archival collection. Where they came from, how old they are, their composition, and use, if any, by primitive people. And yet, the most valuable book on my bookshelf is a book that tells me about the living Stone, the Lord Jesus Christ. The living Stone that was rejected by men. Jesus Christ should be the very cornerstone of our lives, of our very existence.

Let us grab hold of the living Stone, Jesus Christ, upon which we place our hope, our faith, and our trust. Upon this Rock, upon this fortress, we can take refuge in times of trouble. When the storms howl and the winds blow, this Rock will stand the test of time. The very foundations of our lives should be built upon the cornerstone of Christ. It will never give way. It will never crumble. There are no cracks or fault lines in it!

We praise you, God, that you have given us a foundation and a hiding place that will last forever, and ever and ever. Amen.

~ Pastor Robert Lee Long, III

"In my Father's house are many rooms; if it were not so, I would have told you. I am going there to prepare a place for you. And if I go and prepare a place for you, I will come back and take you to be with me that you also may be where I am."

John 14:2-3 (NIV)

A Place For You

The words in this passage from the Gospel of John are comforting at all times, but especially when pondering the passing of a loved one or even our own life after death. Jesus comes to take us "home" to Heaven, when it is our time to go. We do not have to worry about being alone or scared; he is our guide and the one and only way to Heaven.

This knowledge brought me peace as my mother transitioned from this life to the next. I thought, "Jesus is here with her!" She has entered into his presence and taken her place in the eternal house of God. One day, it will be our turn to do the same, and what a glorious day that will be!

Thank you, Lord, that you have made a place for us to spend eternity with you! Amen.

~Ruth Ashcraft Munday

In him [Christ Jesus] and through faith in him we may approach God with freedom and confidence. I ask you, therefore, not to be discouraged because of my sufferings for you, which are your glory.

Ephesians 3:12-13 (NIV)

Approaching God With Freedom And Confidence

The last time my mother went into the hospital, it was determined that we had reached the point that she would go home on hospice. I tried to be strong, to position myself where she would not see the agony on my face, and tried to hold back the tears. Despite my best efforts, little tear-sounds escaped from me…and my Mom asked "Is there a baby in the room?" I answered that yes, it was her baby trying not to snivel and cry, and her response back was immediate and without hesitation: "Stop crying; that's what Heaven is for." Those are words I cherish and will never forget, nor will I forget the wonder and comfort they brought us all.

In her brief words, she was the one offering us consolation and reassurances of God's love for her and for us all. She was encouraging us not to be discouraged, because she had full confidence in God's eternal purpose and knew, despite her many sufferings, that the fullness of God's love and eternal promise was more than enough.

Dear Lord, we know what Heaven is for, yet, we can't help but be sad, too, in hard times. Help us to put our faith and trust in you; knowing that you are with us always and guiding us with your abiding love. Amen.

~Betsy Ashcraft Walker

Jesus replied, "I am the bread of life. Whoever comes to me will never be hungry again. Whoever believes in me will never be thirsty."

John 6:35 (NLT)

Bread That Satisfies

My mother was an excellent cook, along with most all the mothers in Horn Lake in the 50's and 60's. I can still remember her wonderful homemade buttermilk biscuits and the delicious cornbread made from scratch. The banana nut bread that I enjoyed in the home of my friend, however, was my very favorite bread. Ann's mother often sent a generous slice of it to school in her lunch sack, which Ann always shared with me. Through the years, many in the Horn Lake community were blessed with banana nut bread, first through Ann's mother, and later through Ann. I remember that when my mother died in 1997, Ann showed up at my doorstep with banana nut bread. Words weren't necessary; the gift of that sweet bread spoke volumes. My heart was touched and love came softly into my heart and my home.

Jesus Christ described himself as the bread of life. When we receive Jesus as our Lord and Savior, we receive love, joy, peace, and the assurance of Heaven. Will you receive Jesus into your heart and home today? If so, all that is needed is to sincerely pray this prayer:

Jesus, I'm sorry for my sins and ask you to forgive me. I want you to change me to be more like you. I ask that you come into my heart today as Lord and Savior of my life. Amen.

~Carol Little

The Lord is close to the brokenhearted and saves those who are crushed in spirit.

Psalm 34:18 (NIV)

Broken And Crushed

Devastating news—we all receive it at some point in life. A serious illness with a poor prognosis; someone we love is dying. It is never easy to hear. I can remember a day when we had received enough bad news on the health of a loved one, and then more came. So much so, I literally felt crushed in spirit. How do you process endless bad news that breaks your heart in two? This verse from the Psalms spoke to me during those hard days. The words "broken" and "crushed" are quite descriptive, and acknowledge that the Lord understands the level to which we will sometimes hurt. He is with us always, but even more so, when we are too sad for words. He knows our emotions and human fragility. He saves us from the depths of despair. Through his strength, we can get through our trials.

We will come out stronger on the other side—as we have been put back together with God's steadfast love and assurance. His beautiful plan can still take place. You will look back later and marvel how God was with you every step of the way. So if you are feeling "broken" and "crushed" right now, be encouraged, God can and will put you back together in his perfect time.

Thank you, Lord, that you give us your strength to face the days ahead. Amen.

~Ruth Ashcraft Munday

God is our refuge and strength, a very present help in trouble. Therefore will not we fear, though the earth be removed, and though the mountains be carried into the midst of the sea.

Psalm 46:1-2 (KJV)

Can And Will

The words "can" and "will" seem simple enough to understand, but the contemplation of their deeper meaning regarding our faith and hope reveals a bit more about them. "Can" means, of course, "to be able", to have the physical ability or the capacity to do something. "Will" means that we actually choose or desire to do something. God's comfort and strength are always available to us if we can simply remember to look to him and take hold of them, but will we?

We are all grateful to those who have roles that protect and defend all that we hold dear. They are not only well-trained to perform their duties, but they often are called upon to serve in very difficult situations. They can and they will! We are blessed by our Creator to have freedom of choice in how we conduct our lives. Unpleasant matters certainly will come along in our lives, and our challenge will always be to try our best to handle them with courage and grace. These qualities are readily available from the One who is our refuge and our strength. He can, but will we? The choice is ours to make!

Dear Lord, incline our thoughts to you, knowing that we can and will be strengthened and comforted through your abiding power and love. Amen.

~Lee Ashcraft

"Come to me, all you who are weary and burdened, and I will give you rest."

Matthew 11:28 (NIV)

Come

One of my friends has a little girl that likes to say to her playmate of choice, "Come". It is a command with expectation to participate in whatever activity she has in mind. Her eyes shine with excitement as she stands in the doorway, motioning with her little hand.

Similarly, in this passage of scripture, Jesus commands us to "come" to him. We often "play" too long in the cares of this world. Ever been so tired that your eyes won't even close? You may have a glazed-over expression on your face and are functioning on autopilot. Exhausted…body, mind and soul; overwhelmed by life and your current circumstances? If the words "weary" and "burdened" describe you, won't you obey the call and "come" to Jesus today? His invitation is open to all. Give him all your troubles and receive his promise of rest. He is waiting expectantly for you.

Dear Lord, help us to come to you, release our burdens, and receive your promise of rest. Amen.

~Ruth Ashcraft Munday

Because of the Lord's great love we are not consumed, for his compassions never fail. They are new every morning; great is your faithfulness.

Lamentations 3:22-23 (NIV)

Reflections

But the fruit of the Spirit is love, joy, peace, forbearance, kindness, goodness, faithfulness, gentleness and self-control. Against such things there is no law.

Galatians 5:22-23 (NIV)

Cultivating The Fruits Of The Spirit

Many of us are familiar with the Christian camp song about the fruits of the Spirit. It is a very lively and uplifting melody with words taken from this scripture from the Book of Galatians. Not only does the song stir enthusiasm within us, but it also teaches the names of the nine fruits of the Spirit. Learning and internalizing scripture is of great benefit: it strengthens our faith; it increases our knowledge, wisdom, and discernment; it becomes a stored resource for needful times; and it carries us through the most difficult times by providing a solid foundation that we can stand on and hold fast to, no matter what!

To contemplate and meditate on these Christian qualities and characteristics, and to apply them and to be able to reflect their magnificence in our lives, requires a lifetime of dedication. We cannot simply know these nine godly traits, but we must work to live them out daily, even in our most stressful moments. The rewards are truly out of this world!

Dear Lord, we thank you for providing us with such wonderful guidance and comfort. Amen.

~Lee Ashcraft

Then Jesus said to his disciples, "Whoever wants to be my disciple must deny themselves and take up their cross and follow me. For whoever wants to save their life will lose it, but whoever loses their life for me will find it."

Matthew 16:24-25 (NIV)

Denying Ourselves For Jesus

I admit I have never seen this verse in a devotional book about seeking comfort. While Matthew 16:24-25 is not my go-to verse for comfort, I often ponder these words in hindsight and wish I had considered them before praying for comfort. Initially, this verse sounds like the opposite of comfort— yet it is the very command Jesus gives to anyone who wants to live eternally with him.

I am astonished how often I ask for God's comfort, only to be further disappointed when my feelings don't change. I pray for what I see, and not what God sees. I pray for God to change my situation, but I don't change myself. I pray for God to take my burden, yet I won't take up his cross. I easily forget that my temporary happiness is not the reason Jesus died on the cross— Jesus died so we could be free and have an eternal relationship with him.

The next time you go through a challenging time, I hope you will remember this verse and remember what God has first asked of us.

Dear God, we ask for your guidance to allow us to lose ourselves and find comfort through your loving grace. Amen.

~Will Brown

O death, where is thy sting? O grave, where is thy victory? The sting of death is sin; and the strength of sin is the law. But thanks be to God, which giveth us the victory through our Lord Jesus Christ.

1 Corinthians 15:55-57 (KJV)

Departing Triumphantly

At the time that we, or our loved ones, come near to the end of our earthly lives, we surely begin to think about the impending change from life as we know it, to eternal life that we will have in the presence of our Creator. There is no need to fear this transition, because Christ has conquered sin (violation of God's law) and death (the punishment for the violation of God's law) through his own death on our behalf. Through the confidence (faith) that we have in him, we know that we will join him in the heavenly home that has been prepared for us.

The departure from this life has been referred to as "crossing over to the other side", a comforting thought; or, as a time for the "folding of our earthly tent", a reference to the temporary body that our spirit inhabits. We do not have a completely clear image of Heaven, but we have the certainty that the God who set creation in place, who loves us so much that he has made the necessary arrangements for us to join him, will certainly not disappoint us with our eternal reward!

Dear Lord, we thank you for providing for us both now and forever! Amen.

~Lee Ashcraft

Do not be afraid, little flock, for your Father has been pleased to give you the kingdom.

Luke 12:32 (NIV)

I am the good shepherd; I know my sheep and my sheep know me –

John 10:14 (NIV)

Do Not Be Afraid, Little Flock

When you first read this verse, do you immediately notice the intimacy? Isn't it nice to know we are members of God's little flock! "Little" is not a diminishing term here; rather, it implies a small, close group made up of members that each have a personal relationship with each other, and, more importantly, with their shepherd as well.

Jesus uses many references to sheep and their shepherd to help us understand the love God has for us; that we are all flock members known by name! It is very reassuring to know that God provides each of us with that loving and intimate care, and not just for now. He makes us an integral part of his family, with treasures stored up for us in his eternal kingdom.

Thank you, Lord, for shepherding us into your flock and leading us into safe pastures in your eternal kingdom. Help us, along the way, to remember that when we face scary situations, we must listen to your voice and you will guide us through to our heavenly home. Amen.

~Betsy Ashcraft Walker

So do not fear, for I am with you; do not be dismayed, for I am your God. I will strengthen you and help you; I will uphold you with my righteous right hand.

Isaiah 41:10 (NIV)

Do Not Fear

As a little girl, one night I awoke to a blaring alarm in total darkness. My parents were not anywhere I looked! Lost and afraid, I began to cry, and then, in came my Momma! She scooped me up, comforted me and soothingly explained over and over what had occurred (a thunderstorm knocked out power, which also triggered the smoke alarm). Daddy was outside helping a man get his car unstuck from a ditch, and she had gone out to check on Daddy. She reassured me all was well.

After that, thunderstorms scared me. Until I realized that, just like Mom was really always caring for me that night, even if we cannot see God, he IS with us in the chaos of the storm and in our darkest hour. He will not leave us, and even when we do not directly feel it, he is caring for us in the life-events we face. He rejoices with us when we are glad, grieves with us when we are sad, providing peace and comfort always.

So take a deep breath, and trust that God is with you – do not fear – God is guiding you and loving you ALWAYS.

Dear Father, when we feel fearful and afraid, help us to stop and take a deep breath —to know that you are our unfailing strength, with us always in all situations. You can calm or excite us to make it through these challenges. Thank you. Amen.

~Betsy Ashcraft Walker

So we do not lose heart. Even though our outer nature is wasting away, our inner nature is being renewed day by day. For this slight momentary affliction is preparing us for an eternal weight of glory beyond all measure, because we look not at what can be seen but at what cannot be seen; for what can be seen is temporary, but what cannot be seen is eternal.

2 Corinthians 4: 16-18 (NRSV)

Do Not Lose Heart

It is so easy to lose heart and quit. We all have problems in our lives – relationships, work, school, and health—maybe to the point of just walking away or losing heart. Don't let fatigue, pain, or criticism get you down. Don't let the devil get into your head and heart. Renew your commitment to Christ. Don't forsake your eternal reward because of the intensity of today's pain. Your very weakness allows the resurrection power of Christ to strengthen you moment by moment.

Our troubles should not diminish our faith or disillusion us. There is always a purpose in our suffering. There are many benefits that come out of these times: we remember our Lord's suffering for us; we are kept from pride; we look beyond this brief life; we prove our faith to others; and God can take the opportunity to demonstrate his power. Our ultimate hope, when we are experiencing bad/terrible times, is the realization that this life is not all there is. There is life after death for everyone! Where we spend eternity depends upon who we have followed. Knowing we will live forever with God in a place without sin and suffering can help us live above the pain that we face in this life.

Thank you, Lord, for being with us through all of life, especially the tough times. Amen. Be blessed!

~Bro. Ray Owens

But Thomas (who was called the Twin), one of the twelve, was not with them when Jesus came. So the other disciples told him, "We have seen the Lord." But he said to them, "Unless I see the mark of the nails in his hands, and put my finger in the mark of the nails and my hand in his side, I will not believe." A week later his disciples were again in the house, and Thomas was with them.

Although the doors were shut, Jesus came and stood among them and said, "Peace be with you." Then he said to Thomas, "Put your finger here and see my hands. Reach out your hand and put it in my side. Do not doubt but believe." Thomas answered him, "My Lord and my God."

John 20:24-28 (NRSV)

Doubt

The apostle Thomas is often referred to as "doubting Thomas." Rather, could it have been that it was his absence that caused his doubt? Being with other Christians has always helped me through the tough journeys of my life. While Thomas was in denial about the claim of the others that they saw the Lord, we all sometimes live in denial. I'm pretty sure Thomas would not have had this denial had he been present when the Lord appeared to the others.

We don't know why Thomas was absent that day, and he may well have had a good reason. Whatever the reason may have been, his absence caused him to suffer a long week of struggling emotionally and spiritually. The best and surest way and place for us to maintain our faith is to be with our fellow believers.

Lord, when you find us in doubt, may your Spirit awaken us to your loving presence. Amen. Be blessed!

~Bro. Ray Owens

Draw nigh to God, and he will draw nigh to you.

James 4:8a (KJV)

Drawing Nigh To God

Troubled? How close or nigh (near) to God are we? Trying times? Attempting to shoulder the burdens of life alone? No need to! We can simply drop our inhibitions and reach out to, and draw nigh to, our Creator, who knows and loves us, and he will draw nigh to us!

To run with endurance the course set before us (Hebrews 12:1) is a challenge all through life. Special considerations for endurance become even more needful when we must deal with unpleasant situations such as discouraging medical diagnoses or end-of-life realities, but we are never alone! We must increase our faith and avail ourselves of this grace through prayer, knowledge from the scriptures, and fellowship with other Christians. We must only reach for his already outstretched hand!

Dear Lord, help us to put aside all that keeps us from drawing near to you! Amen.

~Lee Ashcraft

"A little faith will bring your soul to Heaven, but great faith will bring Heaven to your soul."

Charles Spurgeon

Reflections

"Peace I leave with you, my peace I give unto you: not as the world giveth, give I unto you. Let not your heart be troubled, neither let it be afraid."

John 14:27 (KJV)

Everlasting Peace

Peace is probably the most desired and sought-after commodity by people anywhere and everywhere. True and lasting peace of mind and heart and soul is available only from God. We all have a yearning to have the vacant spot of our innermost being filled with a satisfying completeness. We often search everywhere for that fulfillment only to discover that it was God all along that we were looking for.

We can prepare for the troubled times in our lives by "pre-loading" that void with the saving grace of a loving God who has been waiting patiently for us to make that most important decision. This is the peace that brings with it comfort and certainty. This is the peace that we can have and keep all through our lives and on into eternity. This is the peace that passes all understanding!

Dear Lord, we thank you for your loving care and your wonderful gift of peace! Amen.

~Lee Ashcraft

For the Lamb at the center of the throne will be their shepherd; he will lead them to the springs of living water. And God will wipe away every tear from their eyes.

Revelation 7:17 (NIV)

Every Tear

This verse from the Book of Revelation shows us that every tear matters. Our pain and sadness here on Earth does not go unnoticed. It is in a tender act of love that God will make all things new in Heaven. We will be with Jesus and there will be no more sorrow or pain.

Let the words from this passage sink in and renew you with hope and comfort today.

Dear Lord, we thank you that you are attentive to our sorrow and know every tear we cry. We praise you that you have given us hope in the promise of making all things new! Amen.

~Ruth Ashcraft Munday

"Fear not, for I have redeemed you; I have summoned you by name; you are mine. When you pass through the waters, I will be with you; and when you pass through the rivers, they will not sweep over you. When you walk through the fire, you will not be burned; the flames will not set you ablaze. For I am the Lord, your God, the Holy One of Israel, your Savior;…Since you are precious and honored in my sight, and because I love you…"

Isaiah 43:1b-3a, 4a (NIV)

Fear Not

These words of God's reassuring love bring so much comfort and strength. They also remind us that God does not promise an unrealistic life of ease. He promises that no matter what (flood, fire, loss, difficult times of all sorts), that he will be WITH US, and through him, we will not be overcome by what we face.

I have been surprised, when I have looked back on heartbreakingly difficult times, to realize how many sweet, but hard, memories I have – those small moments that are evidence of God being with us every step of those sometimes burdensome life journeys. He loves us, and, no matter how grave or dire the situation, he is protectively with us through it all. We can ask for no better gift than his guidance and peace.

Lord, help us to remember that you are with us always; that you love us, have called us by name, and we are yours always. Amen.

~Betsy Ashcraft Walker

Yea, though I walk through the valley of the shadow of death, I will fear no evil: for thou art with me; thy rod and thy staff they comfort me.

Psalm 23:4 (KJV)

Getting Through The Shadowy Places

Shadowy places are characterized by the diminishment or relative absence of light, as in cloudy days or in the early mornings or late evenings. We need light to see clearly and to be able to move about with confidence. Our Lord, the Good Shepherd, the Light of the World, offers that much-needed clarity and confidence to us in all times, and especially in the dark and shadow-filled times of our lives.

He comforts us in such a way that we can journey on along the paths of uncertainty, troubling circumstances, and even impending death with the assurance that he will be with us. We will never have a clear view of what lies ahead as we pass from life as we know it to everlasting life, but we may rest in the thought that he will always be by our side to light the pathway, and we will be drawing even nearer to the One who has always been our Good Shepherd!

Dear Lord, we thank you for being our ever-present source of comfort and guidance in all times! Amen.

~Lee Ashcraft

Are any among you suffering? They should pray. Are any cheerful? They should sing songs of praise. Are any among you sick? They should call for the elders of the church and have them pray over them, anointing them with oil in the name of the Lord. The prayer of faith will save the sick, and the Lord will raise them up; and anyone who has committed sins will be forgiven. Therefore confess your sins to one another, and pray for one another, so that you may be healed. The prayer of the righteous is powerful and effective. Elijah was a human being like us, and he prayed fervently that it might not rain, and for three years and six months it did not rain on the earth. Then he prayed again, and the heaven gave rain and the earth yielded its harvest.

James 5: 13-18 (NRSV)

God Is Good

Around 2005, I began to notice I was having difficulty hearing on the telephone. I have been hard of hearing most of my life, but now it was getting worse. For a Pastor to lose their hearing is devastating. When people are near death and you visit them and listen to them but can't understand what they are saying, it makes it a bad situation. The members of the church for the most part were very understanding.

I remember reading this scripture in the Book of James as a young boy and wondered why God wasn't healing my hearing. I continued to pray and had others to pray for me as well, but my hearing just got worse. I began to use hearing aids and they helped a bit, but my hearing continued to grow worse. Without hearing aids, I hear nothing at all. However, I still have faith that God is with me through this journey and will always be with me. One day I will enter into his presence and my hearing will be perfected. Until that time I will live, as did Paul, with a "thorn in my side".

Lord we thank you for your presence always and will take our thorns as a witness to your great goodness. Amen. Be blessed!

~Bro Ray Owens

"... I am with you always, to the end of the age."

Matthew 28: 20b (NRSV)

God With Us

During a ten-year period in my life, I went through some tough times. From 2005 through 2015, I had kidney stones twice, developed severe rheumatoid arthritis, lost most of my hearing, developed prostate cancer (which later after surgery was told it was stage four, and they could only give me some more time), had both knees replaced, and nearly lost my life when a tree fell on me. My family and church family were such help and blessings during this time of my life.

Above all else, the one constant that I always knew was that the Lord was with me. In the darkest hours of my life, it was this presence of God that took me through the journey, and God continues to be with me to this day. Here I am, now in retirement, and I still trust the Lord to stay with me. When my time to leave this present life comes, I know God will be with me on that journey as well.

Thank you, Lord, for being on our journey with us from beginning to end and especially during our difficult times. Amen. Be blessed!

~Bro Ray Owens

For God so loved the world that he gave his one and only Son, that whoever believes in him shall not perish but have eternal life.

John 3:16 (NIV)

God's Love

As a small child, faithful Sunday School teachers taught me from the Bible that "Jesus loved me". As I grew older, I read for myself John 3:16 and understood that because of God's love for the world, for each one of us, Jesus died on the cross for our sins, and that if we believe in him and ask him to be the Lord and Savior of our lives, that one day we will be with him in Heaven.

As a young mom, when my two-year old son was diagnosed with juvenile rheumatoid arthritis, God brought this same scripture to my mind. As I realized that his Son, Jesus, also suffered, and that my Father in heaven understood how hard this was for me, I was comforted beyond what I would have thought possible. God loves us! Jesus suffered and died for us! Let us thank him for the hope we have for today and for eternity.

Father, thank you for your love for us, and for your son, Jesus, who died for us. Thank you that Jesus is our hope, our anchor, when the storms of life want to overwhelm us. Thank you for the assurance of Heaven. In Jesus' name, Amen.

~Carol Little

And God said, "This is the sign of the covenant I am making between you and every living creature with you, a covenant for all generations to come: I have set my rainbow in the clouds, and it will be a sign of the covenant between me and the earth. Whenever I bring clouds over the earth and the rainbow appears in the clouds, I will remember my covenant between me and you and all living creatures of every kind. Never again will the waters become a flood to destroy all life. Whenever the rainbow appears in the clouds, I will see it and remember the everlasting covenant between God and all living creatures of every kind on the earth."

Genesis 9:12-16 (NIV)

God's Rainbow Covenant

Don't you love to see a rainbow in the sky? This visible reminder of God's covenant love and protection also serves as a gift of reassuring comfort in times of need. For my family, our most memorable rainbow of comfort came at one of the hardest times of our lives: we had just brought my Mom home on hospice, and her body was succumbing to the ravages of end-stage cancer.

During those precious last few days from Christmas into the new year, we had perfect outdoor springtime weather one day; enough to carry Mom out to feel the sunshine on her face for a little while. We had storms that resulted in an amazing double rainbow right over our house that Mom could see from inside in her bed! We had snow! Daffodils, her favorite flower, bloomed early! Your rainbows of comfort may not always be actual rainbows – we can be reminded of God's covenant love for us all in so many different ways, in the smile of a friend or stranger, in the reassuring words from the Bible, through prayer, through a hug, or in the still quiet of our inner heart.

Lord, give us eyes to see your covenant love always, and not just in the rainy times of our lives. We thank you for the beautiful rainbow reminders that you are in covenant with us always. Amen.

~Betsy Ashcraft Walker

"*Our Lord has written the promises of the resurrection, not in books alone, but in every leaf in Springtime.*"

Martin Luther

Reflections

"Lord, if it's you," Peter replied, "tell me to come to you on the water." "Come," he said. Then Peter got down out of the boat, walked on the water and came toward Jesus. But when he saw the wind, he was afraid and, beginning to sink, cried out, "Lord, save me!" Immediately Jesus reached out his hand and caught him. "You of little faith," he said, "why did you doubt?"

Matthew 14:28-31 (NIV)

Immediately

How often do we get caught up in the storms of life and take our eyes off Jesus? Just like Peter, we too may experience the wind of our difficult circumstance whipping around us. We may start to sink into an emotional sea, full of fear and doubt. This causes us to struggle even more, to the point where we feel we might drown trying to make it on our own.

What a comfort to know that all we have to do is cry out to the Lord. He hears us and his response is immediate. He will never leave us or forsake us when we are seeking his saving grace for our lives.

Dear Lord, help us to keep our eyes on you. You are the one who keeps us afloat during the storms of life and will help us overcome the waves of fear and doubt that try to consume us. Thank you that you are the hope of our rescue and immediate source of strength and peace during difficult days. Amen!

~Ruth Ashcraft Munday

You will keep in perfect peace him whose mind is steadfast, because he trusts in you. Trust in the Lord forever, for the Lord, the Lord, is the Rock eternal.

Isaiah 26:3-4 (NIV)

It's Okay

I was working as a Vacation Bible School Leader one year at my home church. One of the little girls in our group had a broken leg. It was in a cast, but she was allowed to walk on it.

She had been carried up the stairs to the lesson room, but she wanted to go back down the stairs on her own. With each step she took, she would say out loud, "it's okay, it's okay", giving herself a pep talk as she went down the stairs. Her words made an impression on me. It was a shining example of child-like faith on how to face a difficult task. As Christians, we can be assured that, whatever happens to us, it will be "okay". If we have our trust in the Lord, he will keep us in perfect peace and is with us each step of the way.

Dear Lord, help us to keep our minds on you and be filled with your perfect peace. Amen

~Ruth Ashcraft Munday

Trust in the Lord with all your heart and lean not on your own understanding; in all your ways acknowledge him and he will make your paths straight.

Proverbs 3:5-6 (NIV)

Lean Not On Your Own Understanding

Proverbs is a book of the Bible that is full of wisdom. My father shared this verse with me many times during my teenage and college years. It has been a favorite scripture that I often refer to even now, in adulthood. Reflecting on this passage has gotten me through many decisions and changing circumstances.

It is easy to get caught up in the "whys" of life. We may not understand all that happens to us. Sometimes, we get impatient and want a fast and easy answer to whatever issue we may be facing. We rush into trying to solve the problem ourselves, instead of waiting on direction from the Lord. Often, we may later regret our choices. Other times, we may be confused over how to handle a problem that seems to have no resolution. These are exactly the instances when we should stop and pray for guidance. The Lord knows our needs and will send the clarity we seek. We need only to follow his command to acknowledge him in every area of our life and trust him with all of our heart.

Dear Lord, please help us to trust you with our whole heart, as we wait on you to guide us through each day. Amen.

~Ruth Ashcraft Munday

The Lord is full of compassion and mercy.

James 5:11c (NIV)

Lessons From Zinnias

My friend, Ann, and I shared a love of zinnias. Actually, we loved all flowers, but zinnias offered a special joy I still share with her family. That shared love of zinnias grew roots with a gentleman who raised zinnias from seeds saved from each year's bloom. With care, his seeds grew and bloomed in a rainbow of bright flowers. Rainbows, whether in light or petals, are pictures of promise and hope.

As zinnias bloom in my summer yard, I often notice a single flower, each a complex masterpiece. What a creation! Neither are we simple. Each of us is a masterpiece, no two alike. We are a mix of so many elements: strengths and weaknesses, thoughts and emotions, insights and concerns, hopes and fears. We are so much more complex than the zinnia…or the lilies of the field…or the sparrow. As are they, we are cared for. Indeed, we are assured that we are loved by a compassionate God—no matter what.

May every flower, every rainbow, every bird, remind of us that we are held in the hands of a compassionate God. Amen.

~Julia Taylor Ebel

"Let not your heart be troubled: ye believe in God, believe also in me."

John 14:1 (KJV)

Letting Our Hearts Not Be Troubled

Easier said than done! The greatest challenge in troubled times can often be to see through and beyond the fog of grief or discouragement. To allow for, to take the time, to make the time, to seek out the grace and peace of our ever-present and loving Savior is absolutely necessary! We need and want the reassurance of his everlasting promise to be with us, to be near us, both now and into eternity! We are not fully equipped to understand the "why" of many things including, certainly, matters of death and eternity, but through our faith, we can endure and continue, encouraged, strengthened, and at peace.

There is great comfort in Dr. Peter Marshall's words: "We believe as Christians, that when our loved ones die, they go to be with the Lord. The Bible teaches that the Lord is with us. Well if they are with him, and he is with us…they cannot be far away."

Dear Lord, we thank you that you are ever-present in all of life's journeys! Amen.

~Lee Ashcraft

And after the earthquake a fire; but the Lord was not in the fire: and after the fire a still small voice.

1 Kings 19:12 (KJV)

Listening For The Still Small Voice

When we are troubled and in need of direction, answers, or solutions, we often become impatient, even to the point of frustration. We want a clear revelation of how to proceed, and we want it delivered right now!

Elijah was waiting for guidance from the Lord, and he likely expected it to be delivered in a mighty way through the great wind, the earthquake, or the fire that came to the mountain where he was hiding. He received the direction he needed from the Lord in the quietness of the time that followed the wind, earthquake, and fire. We too must be still and meditate in prayer and serenity and listen as the gentle, loving voice of hope calms our anxious hearts with answers often delivered in unexpected ways.

Dear Lord, keep our hearts quietly attuned to you and open to receive your direction and assurance! Amen.

~Lee Ashcraft

Love is patient...

I Corinthians 13:4a (NIV)

Love Is Patient

Care-giving for a spouse, parent or grandparent can be very challenging. Managing medication, keeping medical appointments, long waits in crowded doctors' offices, or late nights at the hospital bedside, take their toll on the caregiver. And, the rest of life's demands don't lighten up. Stress builds. Our patience is tested.

However, God is gracious, and will give us the loving patience that care-giving demands, when we call out to him in prayer. Treasure every moment with your loved one, and thank the Lord you're able to help them in their greatest time of need.

Father, bless the caregivers, give them the strength and loving patience they need. Amen.

~Greg Munday

"No longer do I call you servants, for the servant does not know what his master is doing; but I have called you friends ….."

John 15:15 (ESV)

My Precious Ann

I met my friend, Ann, the first day of first grade at Horn Lake School. We quickly became best friends and remained best friends until she passed away from cancer. Ann loved Jesus with all her heart and attended Horn Lake United Methodist Church where she served faithfully her entire life. Children were her heart, so at every opportunity she poured into them biblical truths that would sustain them throughout their lives.

She was a wonderful daughter, wife and mother; but for me, she was a true friend who could be trusted, counted on, and was always ready to lend a hand. She loved me through thick and thin, through all the seasons of our lives, and I loved her. Her friendship speaks to me of the friendship that Jesus desires to have with each of us, if only we will ask him.

Jesus, I ask you today to be my everlasting friend. Thank you for your love which sustains me, comforts me, and endures forever. Amen.

~Carol Little

"Trials are not enemies of faith but are opportunities to prove God's faithfulness."

Author Unknown

Reflections

For God has not given us a spirit of fear and timidity, but of power, love, and self-discipline.

2 Timothy 1:7 (NLT)

This is my command – be strong and courageous! Do not be afraid or discouraged. For the Lord your God is with you wherever you go.

Joshua 1:9 (NLT)

Not A Spirit Of Fear

A high-risk pregnancy was followed by a normal delivery, and my beautiful child was placed in my arms. However, my mother's intuition told me something was not right. After months of concern, it was determined there was a problem, big enough to require extensive and delicate surgery. Deep worry, fear, and anxiety came pouring down.

I had recalled 2 Timothy many times in life and remembered it again in this moment. Through every fear, trial, heartache, and suffering, there is the gift of the Holy Spirit, which never leaves us. Whatever fear you may be facing today, God asks for you to give it to him, so that he can and will work all things together for his glory.

As a parent, I understand that I want to provide the best and what is good and right to my own children. As a child of God, I sense his love for me in this same way, yet it is infinitely bigger, better, and beyond anything I could ever know! There is no greater gift than his love for us.

Thank you, Lord, that you are always with us! You give us strength to overcome our fears during difficult times! Amen.

~Amanda Lane

His master said to him, "Well done, good and trustworthy slave; you have been trustworthy in a few things, I will put you in charge of many things; enter into the joy of your master."

Matthew 25:21 (NRSV)

Our Heavenly Reward

Of all the things I could hear from the Lord when I enter his presence, this will be the most meaningful: that I have lived my life in such a way that it has made a difference for others, for myself, and for the Lord. As a Pastor, I have been with many when they face their final journey home; the thing I always want to be able to say is that you will soon hear the words from this scripture from the one who has paid the ultimate price for your salvation.

As we have lived our lives, we have been blessed in many ways by the Lord. Some of the blessings we have realized for what they are; others we may have not even known. As we hear these words from our Lord, we will know that we have arrived to our eternal home and will live forever with the Lord from that moment on. Let us remember that we are already living with him on this earth in Spirit – soon we will live with him, and all those who have gone before us, in our heavenly body.

We thank you Lord for life here and look forward to life in your presence. Amen. Be blessed!

~Bro. Ray Owens

Rejoice always; pray without ceasing; give thanks in all circumstances; for this is the will of God in Christ Jesus for you. Do not quench the Spirit.

1 Thessalonians 5:16-19 (ESV)

Perpetual Prayer And Thanksgiving

Our lives are overwhelmingly busy and can bring on unbearable tasks. During difficult tasks, let us challenge the feelings of doubt and fear, and, instead, be encouraged. Rejoice in God's unfailing love; in his goodness and grace, and, rejoice in his perfect plan. Rejoicing brings our awareness to the many miracles throughout our days, yet giving us more reasons to rejoice!

Pray, through the trials, during the mundane, and even while rejoicing. Praying consistently leads us to rely completely on God, leaving us to rest in his peaceful presence and drawing us closer to him.

Give thanks! We are most thankful when our lives are full of ease and good fortune. However, during the difficult times, say a prayer of thanksgiving and find a brighter outlook by recognizing the many blessings we have been given.

Follow God's direction and find peace and contentment in him. Know that when difficult paths arise, God has not planned this to punish or hurt our earthly bodies and hearts, but to prepare our eternal bodies for him.

Gracious Father, help us to trust in your plan and focus only on your light. Shield us with your love so we may have the courage to continue in a way that is pleasing to you. Amen.

~Jessica James Pounders

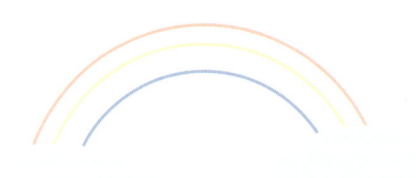

Now to him who is able to do immeasurably more than all we ask or imagine, according to his power that is at work within us…

Ephesians 3:20 (NIV)

Positive Ways To Channel Grief

After the loss of a loved one, we often find ourselves searching for ways to stay connected to them. We no longer have their physical presence, but we desire to be close to them in spirit. My family and I have started several projects (including this book) in tribute to my mother, Ann. It helps to be able to talk or write about her and the type of life she lived, sharing God's love with everyone she met.

The Lord has blessed beyond measure the activities we have undertaken to celebrate her life. Maybe you are struggling right now with how to handle the void left by that certain someone. Consider taking up a cause they firmly believed in doing, writing about their story, or starting up a ministry to help those in need, using your loved one's name. Whatever it is, find a positive way to channel your grief. It may seem difficult right now, but the Lord will begin to work his healing spirit in you, as you seek to serve others.

Thank you, Lord, that you are at work in our lives, changing our grief into a testimony of your glory! Amen.

~Ruth Ashcraft Munday

Pray without ceasing. In everything give thanks: for this is the will of God in Christ Jesus concerning you.

1 Thessalonians 5:17-18 (KJV)

Pray Without Ceasing, Giving Thanks

The silent prayers and uplifted thoughts of our minds and hearts reach God without even being completely verbalized or carefully organized. Our Creator knows our needs even when we find it difficult to express them! Our cares and worries, especially the impending loss of a loved one, can make us lose focus on the nearness of God, his comfort, and the very peace of mind that he offers.

We must always consider the needs of all concerned, and not just ourselves, since grieving can be different for everyone, but ALL can be made stronger in his grace and peace through prayer and thanksgiving. In this scripture, we are reminded to be thankful IN all circumstances (not necessarily FOR all circumstances) because we have a loving God to see us through every experience in life!

Dear Lord, we thank you for the peace that you bring to our lives through the reassurances of your love and care that we find in all that surrounds us daily. Amen.

~Lee Ashcraft

For ye have need of patience, that, after ye have done the will of God, ye might receive the promise.

Hebrews 10:36 (KJV)

Proceeding On With Untenuous Tenacity

We all certainly have many needs in our lives: the need to be loved and accepted; the basic needs of all for food, clothing, and shelter; and the need to be of service to our fellow man. The most important need of all though is to have a close and personal relationship with Jesus Christ. We would all agree that it takes time and patience to cultivate friendships and affection, even with those who are in the circles nearest to us. The need to be of service and show compassion to others is a gift, and one that requires us to rise above ourselves, to take the high road, even when we may be weary or dismayed.

If we have, and we must have, above all, the commitment to pattern our lives after Christ, then we are empowered to patiently serve, and to endure, and to ultimately triumph over all that we encounter in our journey through life. By showing courage in our faith, especially in difficult situations, we encourage others to do likewise, and we can continue on to receive the promise, the promise of eternal life in the presence of God!

Dear Lord, fill us with the courage to do your will in our lives, and with the grace and peace to understand and receive your promise! Amen.

~Lee Ashcraft

Set me as a seal upon your heart, as a seal upon your arm; for love is as strong as death...

Song of Solomon 8:6a (ESV)

Set God's Love As A Seal

Until you experience the deep grief associated with a long separation, or even more, with the loss of a close loved one in your life, these words may simply sound romantic, which they are; I even had these words sung at my wedding! However, after experiencing the deep loss of my maternal grandparents, my mother and my aunt, in an all-too-brief span of time, these words now have a more profoundly comforting meaning.

After my mother passed away, I did not feel her love any less than I did before; not in my heart. I could not feel her physical demonstrations of love, but it abides there in my heart, unvanquished by death or time, because it was and is sealed in.

If our ever-abiding love for each other as humans is "as strong as death," then how much stronger is God's love for us? God's love is his greatest gift to us – and it is set as a seal, a promise and a sign, for us on our hearts, and that is a power that overcomes death, and any defeat, every time.

Lord, we thank you that your seal is love and that it is as strong as death, so we know it is eternal. Help us to remember that while separation in this life is hard, eternal love and reunion await us under your great seal. Amen.

~Betsy Ashcraft Walker

Therefore, as God's chosen people, holy and dearly loved, clothe yourselves with compassion, kindness, humility, gentleness and patience.

Colossians 3:12 (NIV)

Small Acts Of Kindness

Rushing to work one morning, I had to make a quick stop at a gas station to add some air to one of my car's front tires. Just as I was steering to the station's free air pump, a driver in a 4X4 pickup carrying an ATV four wheeler in its bed pulled in a split second ahead of me.

I got out of my car, leaned against the hood, and as I folded my arms I thought, "Well great, I'm late for work and now I'll have to wait while this fellow probably spends the next 20 minutes putting air in all those tires."

But the gentleman did something I didn't expect. He picked up the air nozzle, walked over to me, and with a polite nod, handed it to me. He didn't say a word, just stepped back and seemed perfectly content with allowing me to go ahead of him.

A rushed, hectic morning, turned a bit brighter for me because someone took the time to be kind.

Often, it is the case that just a small act of kindness, given unselfishly by one of God's own, is all it takes to make someone's day a little better.

Dear Lord, help us extend kindness to others, as a reflection of your love and grace in our lives. Amen.

~Greg Munday

*Cast all your anxiety on him
because he cares for you.*

1 Peter 5:7 (NIV)

Reflections

May the Lord answer you when you are in distress…
Some trust in chariots and some in horses, but we trust in
the name of the Lord our God.

Psalm 20: 1a and 7 (NIV)

Some Trust In Chariots

Perhaps you are just entering into a season of grief or very hard situations; perhaps you are recovering from such difficult periods. One of the gifts that comes out of hard times, like a rainbow after a storm, is the ability to empathize with others going into or through similar situations. The loss of someone beloved to you leaves a permanent change upon you – but it doesn't have to be an inhibiting change.

Through the difficulties of a hard diagnosis, an unwanted prognosis, a lengthy illness, an unexpected tragedy, or other long-endured difficulties, we find in ourselves an inner strength that we might otherwise have overlooked. We do what must be done; we proceed on; we endure. This is possible through the hope we have in God, the trust we have in our faith and salvation, and God's unwavering love for us all. Place your trust in the Lord, and prepare to be amazed at what you CAN do through him and what he can do through you! In doing so, you help others to see God's rainbows of comfort AND experience them again yourself!

Lord, we don't like the hard times, but we take heart in your peace that passes understanding, your calming presence, and your uplifting strength. Help us to be your vessel to share those gifts with others in need as well. Amen.

~Betsy Ashcraft Walker

O Lord, how manifold are your works!

Psalm 104:24a (NRSV)

The Gift Of Beauty

For you caregivers, loved ones, friends—you who offer support to those who face life's weights, challenges, or dimming futures—this message is simple: Remember beauty, wherever it can be found, wherever it has been shared.

Beauty can be as complex as masterpieces of art, music, and architecture or as simple as a daffodil, bird song, or rainbow. Beauty speaks in the fluttering butterfly or darting hummingbird, in a whisper of wind across a distant hill, in the hush of snow.

How can you capture beauty to share where it might lift spirits? Can you share photographs of nature or loved ones? Can you shape beauty in words—a simple poem that creates a snapshot, a spoken image of a beautiful sky? Can you gather fragrant beauty in lilacs? Can you share beauty in soft moss, silky yarn, a puppy's fur… the taste of freshly baked bread…a gentle word, a soft touch, or sweet memories?

Beauty feeds our souls and souls of those we love, in both bright moments and dark ones. Share beauty.

May our eyes and hearts be open to beauty around us, and may that beauty nourish our souls and the souls of those we love. Amen.

~Julia Taylor Ebel

*The Lord your God is with you, he is mighty to save.
He will take great delight in you, he will quiet you with
his love, he will rejoice over your with singing.*

Zephaniah 3:17 (NIV)

The Gift Of Song

Having grown up in a musical family, songs have always been a source of inspiration and comfort to me. Hymns have words of strength that provide encouragement, often coming to mind right when you need them. Or, perhaps a song on the radio may speak to you. Sometimes, I like to play a song over and over again, if it fits my circumstance, taking the words to heart.

My mother, Ann, loved to sing, and was blessed with a lovely voice. She would go around humming throughout the day; when it came time to do household chores, she could often be found belting out a tune as she vacuumed. Music carried her through her life, all the way to the end. It was a gift from God. The Bible contains many references to singing. Songs of praise and thanksgiving are acts of worship, lifting our spirits as we focus on God, instead of our troubles. Music serves as a beautiful link between Heaven and Earth, connecting us with yet another glimpse of what those who have gone before us may be experiencing. May thoughts of loved ones surrounded by heavenly music and unconditional love, bring comfort and peace to you.

Thank you Lord for the gift of song! Let us reflect on the words and the music that you place within our hearts and minds to help us find comfort during difficult times. Amen.

~Ruth Ashcraft Munday

The Lord gives strength to his people; the Lord blesses his people with peace.

Psalm 29:11 (NIV)

The Gifts Of Strength And Peace

I have this verse taped to my bathroom mirror. It is there to greet me every morning when I am drying my hair and preparing for the day ahead. This scripture became a comfort to me during a difficult time when one of my grandparents was in the hospital. It was a lengthy hospitalization and fraught with multiple concerns. My family and I were taking rotating shifts at the bedside, so that someone was always there, as well as someone caring for the other grandparent at home. We were all tired and concerned about the outcome of these circumstances. I would work, go to the hospital, take a shift as a caregiver, swap out with another family member, go home, sleep, and then repeat the same routine the next day.

One co-worker asked me, "How are you able to keep up this schedule while remaining so calm and focused?" My response was, "I don't know—it's not my own strength. God is getting us through." I truly felt we all had been blessed with an extra "helping" of strength and peace that comes only from the Lord. He knows just what we need when the going gets tough.

Thank you, Lord, for the gifts of strength and peace; they carry us through difficult circumstances, drawing us closer to you. Amen.

~Ruth Ashcraft Munday

The Lord is my strength and my shield; my heart trusts in him, and I am helped.

Psalm 28:7a (NIV)

The Lord Is My Strength

To fight a good battle with a sword and shield you need strength, agility, disciplined training, and confidence in your battle gear. In modern times, the encounters we face may not be literally sword-and-shield type battles, but they do still have the same requirements. With God as our strength and shield, we can be at ease that he is our help in all situations and will be with us through the fight.

Throughout the Bible, we are reminded that God does not promise us a challenge-free world or life, but instead, provides us with what we need to face the challenges encountered. He prepares us through prayer, his word, his love and his Holy Spirit for every life battle we face.

God, we do not always understand why we have to fight the battles of our lives, but we do take heart that you are our strength and shield in all scenarios. Give us your peace and assurance to know that even in the best or worst of life, you ARE our shield. Help us to draw strength from you when our own has failed and we feel discouraged, heartbroken, hopeless or alone. Give us solace through your word and your people to know that under your shield we are never alone and your strength and support will never fail us; thank you. Amen.

~ Betsy Ashcraft Walker

And the peace of God, which surpasses all understanding, will guard your hearts and your minds in Christ Jesus.

Philippians 4:7 (NRSV)

The Peace Of God

January 17, 2015, was a life-changing day for me. While someone was cutting a huge oak tree that measured 42" in diameter and 110' tall, it fell on me. Lying under that tree I remember it being so dark. I couldn't breathe, and my head felt like it would burst at any moment. I couldn't understand at first what was happening, and I began yelling for someone to get it off of me. Then I remembered—I was running from the tree and it caught me. At that moment, I felt the presence of God and all fear left me, and I was at peace. I was looking for the light leading me to the Lord, but when the light came, I was still in the world. The doctors told my family they didn't think I would survive, but God had other plans.

During nine months of hospital stay and then rehabilitation, I was able to return to my new life. I wasn't completely the same as before. As the rehab folks said, "This is your new normal." Today, I continue in my new normal. During all this time, God has been with us, keeping his promise of peace.

Thank you, Lord, for your peace that surpasses all understanding. Amen. Be blessed!

~Bro. Ray Owens

Blessed are those who mourn, for they will be comforted.

Matthew 5:4 (NIV)

The Promise Of Comfort

At some point in our lives, we all experience loss. Maybe it is the loss of a loved one. Or, perhaps, it is the loss of health, an unfulfilled dream, an unexpected career change, or something else in life that did not go as you planned. Each of these circumstances may cause us to mourn for what we no longer have.

If you are grieving right now, read and reread this passage from the Book of Matthew. It is a blessing with a promise, and the promise is real. Comfort may seem slow in coming, but, in time, it will happen. The Lord always keeps his word.

Dear Lord, thank you that you have given me the promise of comfort. Help me to release my sadness and loss to you today, so that your healing may begin within me. Amen.

~Ruth Ashcraft Munday

Then he said, "Jesus, remember me when you come into your kingdom." Jesus answered him, "I tell you the truth, today you will be with me in paradise."

Luke 23:42-43 (NIV)

Today

As we are considering many matters surrounding end-of-life for ourselves or for loved ones, there is great comfort to be drawn from this scripture. The conversation between Jesus and this thief on the cross should provide affirmation for us that, up until our final breath, it is never too late to acknowledge Jesus as our Lord and Savior.

No matter what is in our past or what we may have done even yesterday, today it is possible to make a new start. Choose Jesus; receive the gift of salvation, forgiveness, and his promise of eternal life.

Thank you, Lord, that you offer us forgiveness and grace. Your promise of eternal life, for those who acknowledge you as their Lord and Savior, is what we place our hope in today. Amen.

~Ruth Ashcraft Munday

...but those that hope in the Lord will renew their strength. They will soar on wings like eagles; they will run and not grow weary, they will walk and not be faint.

Isaiah 40:31 (NIV)

Reflections

Friends come and friends go, but a true friend sticks by you like family.

Proverbs 18: 24 (MSG)

Most of all, love each other as if your life depended on it. Love makes up for practically anything.

1 Peter 4:8 (MSG)

True Friends

My phone names the sound "Opener"—it sounds like a bottle being opened and the cap bouncing across the table. This is notification that I have a new message in a group chat I have with some of my friends—brothers in ministry whom I've known for decades. This group text keeps us in contact despite the physical distance between us.

When I hear the "Opener" sound, I never know what the message will be. Sometimes it's a prayer, or prayer request. It may be a scripture verse, an inspirational quote, or a corny joke. We check up on each other, encourage one another, plan future adventures, and ask for and give advice. They are there for me in the tough times, and I try to be there for them.

These friends are like family; I thank God for them. I know I can count on them. The love and support of these brothers in faith during tough times reminds me that God is always with me, no matter what I face.

Thank you, Lord, for all of those who love and care for me. They remind me of your love and grace. Amen.

~Rev. David Huffman

Wait for the Lord; be strong and take heart and wait for the Lord.

Psalm 27:14 (NIV)

Wait For The Lord

How hard waiting is! In stressful situations, especially, we feel as if we must be doing something, even if there is nothing to do. Whether waiting on potentially life-changing news or something quite simple, we are encouraged to be strong in the Lord and to take heart. It can also be a time of preparation of things yet to come or reconsideration of things before. Sometimes waiting can make us stop and rest. Resting in the Lord is vital to our spiritual well-being, lending strength and courage during our greatest times of need. Waiting and resting is a way of sustaining our physical and spiritual strength.

There are times in our lives when we are the ones directly going through an ordeal; there are other times when we are *with* someone else going through the direct difficulties. Remember that our ever-source of help is God – through his love for us in Jesus and the Holy Spirit, he is with us, even when we feel alone; God is waiting on us to wait on him.

Remember that our timing is not God's timing. Seek God's timing, so that you stand not ahead or behind him, but with him.

Heavenly Father, we thank you for waiting for us; give us your strength and courage to face the hard days ahead; give us your joy and laughter to celebrate the good as well. Amen.

~Betsy Ashcraft Walker

In the morning, O Lord, you hear my voice; in the morning I lay my requests before you and wait in expectation.

Psalm 5:3 (NIV)

Waiting In Expectation

One week before my 41st birthday, I was laid off from a job I had (mostly) enjoyed for 11 years. After the shock and initial emotions had eased, I was faced with something I hadn't fully appreciated before: time.

It would have been easy to use that time to worry about the job search, how I was going to pay the bills, if I would need to sell my house, and whether people thought I was somehow to blame for being laid off. To be honest, all those things happened, but I refused to wallow in the "what ifs" too much. Instead, I learned to treasure the time I had – to sleep, to let my body and mind recover from a stressful job, to store up memories with family, and to spend time with God.

In a season of uncertainty, faith becomes even more important. In Psalm 5:3, David wrote, "In the morning I lay my requests before you and wait in expectation." Waiting in expectation isn't passive. It's an act of trust, of believing that God is going to act.

When you don't know what's coming, trust the One who never changes. Know that he loves you. Believe that he is at work. Wait in expectation.

Father, when I feel lost, help me to remember that you can always be trusted. Amen.

~Lori Jean Mantooth

After six days Jesus took with him Peter, James and John the brother of James, and led them up a high mountain by themselves. There he was transfigured before them. His face shone like the sun, and his clothes became as white as the light. Just then there appeared before them Moses and Elijah, talking with Jesus. Peter said to Jesus, "Lord, it is good for us to be here. If you wish, I will put up three shelters—one for you, one for Moses and one for Elijah."

Matthew 17:1-4 (NIV)

We Will Recognize Them

This is a lengthy passage, but one I find filled with hope and comfort. It provides a glimpse of what we might see in Heaven. Through this description, it appears we will be able to recognize those who have gone before us. If Peter, James, and John were able to recognize Moses and Elijah, who they had never met, let that inspire you.

Thoughts of reuniting with our loved ones, and also greeting those we have never met, create a warm image that should cast out any fear we might have about the mysteries of eternity. We are, and will continue to be, one big family of God. We may not understand all about Heaven, but we can be at peace knowing we will be seeing the Lord, our loved ones, and multiple believers we did not have the pleasure of meeting here on Earth.

Lord, we thank you for this glimpse of your glory. Fill our hearts and minds with the assurance that comes from knowing you. We are grateful that you extend an invitation of grace to everyone, to become a part of your eternal family. Amen.

~Ruth Ashcraft Munday

May the God of hope fill you with all joy and peace in believing, so that by the power of the Holy Spirit you may abound in hope.

Romans 15:13 (ESV)

What A Hope We Have!

When my mother passed away in 2010, after a long battle with cancer, I was devastated. There are still times that I miss her so much it makes me cry. But the moment she left this earth to go to her forever home in heaven, I immediately knew I would see her again one day. A *"hope"* sprang up in me that I had never experienced before.

I have carried that *"hope"* through the years since her death, and as my Daddy approached the end of his life this past winter, I held on to that *"hope"* even tighter.

On those days when I miss them so much it hurts, the God of *"hope"* gently reminds me that HE is my *"hope"*, and that in a blink of his eye, we'll be together again.

Dear Lord, thank you that you are the source of our "hope". Through your divine plan, we have the opportunity to spend eternity with you and see our loved ones again! Amen.

~ Heather McCullar Myrick

Then God said, "Let us make man in our image, in our likeness…".

Genesis 1:26 (NIV)

What Does God Look Like?

Have you ever wondered what God looks like? What do you need to see what God looks like? Here it is: a mirror. If, we are made in God's likeness, all we need to do is look in the mirror at our own face to see God's glory, to look in the faces of those around us to see God's splendor, and to see God in us, at work in our lives.

We all must remember that we are God's children and should reflect not only his image, but his LOVE, to all bearing his image—all people on Earth. Sometimes it is hard to feel loving, to show love, or to receive love. On your best or worst day, remember that you don't need a super hero shield, you don't need a fancy title or super powers, you need a kind eye, a loving smile, and a loving heart to see, reflect, and share God's love all around you.

Give us your eyes to see you, your face to reflect you, your arms to reach out for you, and your heart for love. Help us to remember, when we feel that we have nothing left to give, we have you in us and with us ALWAYS in your abiding love. Help us to see this love in ourselves and to share it and receive it with those around us. Amen.

~ Betsy Ashcraft Walker

The Lord is my rock, and my fortress, and my deliverer; my God, my strength, in whom I will trust; my buckler, and the horn of my salvation, and my high tower.

Psalm 18:2 (KJV)

Whelmed, But Not Overwhelmed

When the whelming floods of life cause us to struggle with fear, doubt, confusion, and dismay, we can find buoyancy and courage and be lifted to higher ground by remembering to keep our faith strong, and our hope sure, that we will emerge well-fortified and ever closer to our Lord and Creator. Just as this Psalmist, David, wrote, we can find strength to continue on, despite our circumstances, when we refuse to be overwhelmed, but instead allow our Lord to shield us, to save us, to comfort us, and to keep us secure with him by seeking his presence in the loftiest places within our hearts and minds and souls.

There is no depth so low or height so great that we cannot find the love of God always present. Just as David and his armies knew, and even armies today know, there is great advantage in seeking the high ground. Perspective, strength, comfort, and deliverance are ours when we take hold of the Most High and Solid Rock!

Dear Lord, we thank you for your presence and faithfulness to us in all of the days and times of our lives! Amen.

~Lee Ashcraft

In the same way, the Spirit helps us in our weakness. We do not know what we ought to pray for, but the Spirit himself intercedes for us through wordless groans. And he who searches our hearts knows the mind of the Spirit, because the Spirit intercedes for God's people in accordance with the will of God. And we know that in all things God works for the good of those who love him, who have been called according to his purpose.

Romans 8:26-28 (NIV)

When There Are No Words

In 2012, my 4-year-old daughter was diagnosed with an aggressive brain tumor. Such a diagnosis is life-altering for the whole family, but for me as a mother, watching my child live near death's door changed me forever.

Being the mother of a sick child awakened a response in me to be super mom. I found myself constantly trying to grab onto some sort of control over the situation only to be reminded time after time that ultimately I was not in control. I found comfort in knowing that in my weakest moments, when I had no strength, the words of my prayers had run dry and the ache of my heart was all I had left, the Spirit was interceding to God on my behalf.

Ava is now 11 years old and 3 years cancer free. Even though cancer has left holes in our lives, it has also provided doors I never could have seen. I still pray for his will to be done. Fear is an emotion Satan loves to use in our family. He knows we are concerned that the cancer may come back, but we continue to pray even when there are no words to describe the pain and fear.

Thank you, Lord, that you know our needs and hear our prayers, even when there are no words. Amen.

~Rebecca Roten

As the rain and the snow come down from Heaven, and do not return to it without watering the earth and making it bud and flourish, so that it yields seed for the sower and bread for the eater, so is my word that goes out from my mouth: It will not return to me empty, but will accomplish what I desire and achieve the purpose for which I sent it.

Isaiah 55:10-11 (NIV)

Reflections

Quotation Reference and Bible Permissions

Scripture quotations marked KJV are from the King James Version of the Bible.

Scripture quotations marked NRSV are from the New Revised Standard Version Bible, 1989, The Division of Christian Education of the National Council of Churches of Christ in the United States of America. Used by permission. All rights reserved.

Scripture quotations marked NLT are taken from the Holy Bible. New Living Translation copyright© 1996, 2004, 2007 by Tyndale House Foundation. Used by permission of Tyndale House Publishers, Inc. Carol Stream, Illinois 60188. All rights reserved.

Scripture quotations marked ESV are from the English Standard Version ®. Copyright ©2001 by Crossway Bibles, a division of Good News Publishers. Used by permission.

Scriptures quotations marked NIV are taken from the Holy Bible. New International Version ®, NIV®.Copyright © 1973, 1978, 1984, 2011 by Biblica, Inc.™ Used by permission of Zondervan. All rights reserved worldwide. www.zondervan.com The "NIV" and "New International Version" are trademarks registered in the United States Patent and Trademark Office by Biblica, Inc. ™

Scripture quotations marked MSG are from The MESSSAGE REMIX: The Bible in Contemporary Language. Scripture taken from THE MESSAGE Copyright©1993, 1994, 1995, 1996, 2000, 2001, 2002. Used by permission of NavPress Publishing Group.

Quotations from Peter Marshall ,Charles Spurgeon, Martin Luther and Unknown Author are from Bless Your Heart Samples from the Heartland, Copyright ©1987 Mary Bevis and Nini Sieck.